call to the
streets

Harry —
God bless you as
you answer the call

Don Williams

call to the streets

DON WILLIAMS

AUGSBURG PUBLISHING HOUSE
MINNEAPOLIS, MINNESOTA

CALL TO THE STREETS

contents

preface

This book presents the major events in my ministry in Hollywood in the last five years as the "Jesus Movement" has emerged about us and, in part, through us. It is a call for some cultural and historical understanding and a new and radical response by the organized church to these unconventional Christians.

I cannot send this to press without expressing deep gratitude to the leadership and membership of the First Presbyterian Church of Hollywood for their support and faithfulness as a new and often risky ministry unfolded for us. Whenever the chips were down the session voted "yes"—and money, love, and prayers were forthcoming.

Dr. Raymond I. Lindquist, our senior pastor, has been a father to me in the gospel, a source of unfailing encouragement and inspiration. His grace and charm have been complemented by the wisdom and openness that the church so desperately needs today. John Haman served as president of the board of directors of our church when the Salt Company was built. His tireless energy and Christian optimism made this experiment in communication humanly possible, and he is a dear brother and friend to me. Many others have worked largely behind the scenes to support our street ministry and drug rehabilitation programs. Louis Hahn, Guy Martin, Eric Jeffries, Fred Grayston, Bob Reed, Bob Toms, Phil Licht, Bob Munger, Ken Skinner, Biff Oliver, Bob Matthews, Tim McCalmont, Bob Buchanan, and Dennis Lampson are only a few to whom my special thanks in Christ goes.

My thanks also to Evelyn Skinner for permission to quote from her heart-breaking and heart-warming story, "Christ Still Works Miracles," and to the editor of *Christianity Today* for permission to use parts of my article, "Close-up of the Jesus People" (Vol. XV, Number 23, August 27, 1971). My thanks as well to Dr. Karl Olsson and Dr. Milton Engebretson for the invitation to address the theological conference of the International Federation of Free Evangelical Churches on "Ministries Among the Jesus People" in Chicago, September, 1971. The substance of those talks appear in this book.

The writing of this manuscript has been during a voyage into Alaskan waters aboard the *M. V. Malaspina* accompanied by my dear brother and friend Gary Zentmyer, co-worker in the gospel. The beauties of an untouched coastline have accentuated both the original creation as God intended it and the haunting tragedy and cry of this generation for reality. It is in response to that cry that the Jesus Movement has exploded upon us, and we have ventured forth in new forms of ministry.

1

the opening doors

I had just preached the eleven o'clock service, and she stood, staring at the floor, crying softly. She was waiting for me to finish greeting the congregation, and I felt an uneasy concern as I smiled and squeezed the hands held out to me.

We were alone now in the vast sanctuary, and the red eyes and mascara smears pled for help. I suggested we go back behind the pulpit to the robing room where the problem was quickly revealed. Cheryl had lived for two years on the Sunset Strip. Now in June of 1967 she was a broken girl, pregnant and alone. She had put on her only dress and struggled into the biggest church she could find

to be lost to all but God. Somehow the message had touched her. She was surprised to see a young man in the pulpit, and this gave her enough confidence to make her move. "I'm too guilty," she confessed softly, "God could never forgive me." My memory reached back for old Bible verses learned in my early Christian life—the promise of forgiveness and cleansing. The words came easily and honestly. What counsel could I give this abused girl? God's counsel; nothing more.

In twenty minutes it was over—and just beginning. We prayed, and now Cheryl could look me in the eye. She blew her nose, smiled slightly, and assured me that she would return to the evening service.

Back she came that night with Michelle, her roommate. When I dropped them off at their apartment later Cheryl turned to me as she stepped from the car and said, "For the first time I'm not alone." In a new way I wasn't alone either; Cheryl was about to take me into a new world of the streets: coffee houses, drugs, long hairs, the age of Aquarius. My ministry would not be the same again.

●

He was a good looking kid with his Jerry West haircut and dapper clothes, but his face told me of his hurt before he opened his mouth. He came to church for a few weeks, and I sensed he was trying to get close to me. Finally, I said, "Bob, let's go out for dinner." There his story emerged.

A mother who had a string of boyfriends and a thirst for alcohol had abandoned him in junior high

school. He was taken in by a matriarchal Moses who ran her Christian home by the rules. Here physical provision was made and performance produced without emotional satisfaction. The hurt and loneliness were never healed. Three years of parochial high school were rewarded with a baseball and basketball scholarship to one of the better Christian liberal arts colleges near Santa Barbara.

"Ten chapel cuts and you're out." By the spring, Bob had managed this and returned to Los Angeles in debt and bitter.

Athletics had held him together through adolescence. Now they were gone. Drugs weren't heavily on the scene yet, and Bob's mother had gifted him with an aversion to alcohol. One night the hole was filled, at least for the present. A friend offered a ticket to a concert at the Santa Monica Civic Auditorium, and as Bob sat in the second row center another Bob stepped on the stage with an acoustical guitar and harmonicas. That Bob? Bob Dylan. His simple melodies and complex words gripped the attention and criticized, but never satisfied. The endless images sent the mind reeling and stumbling. The moods constantly shifted—idealism, pathos, love found and lost, and the quest, ever the quest. War, racism, materialism, pride were probed like tumors fingered by a skilled surgeon.

Now the younger Bob got his guitar and harmonicas and took me into the world of folk and folk rock. Being in my Ray Conniff era, at first I felt as if I were being subjected to a weird Chinese torture. Then the melodies caught, and beyond the nasal, rough, and thin voice of Dylan I heard genius. What

13

I saw on the streets with Cheryl, I heard from the music of Bob. Once more, my ministry was never to be the same again.

●

Lance walked in with freaky clothes and a giant red beard, a smile on his round face and his hands in his pockets. His image said, "unconventional." He was. A Christian home had given him the basics of the faith, but like so many of his generation he had to "do his own thing," at least for a while. Lance was an artist. Artists are allowed to experiment, to feel life. He did. Lance's asthma made drugs available by prescription, and it was easy to abuse the new freedom the culture offered, but the family foundation drew him back to church. After getting "wired" on his asthma pills on Saturday night, he would make church on Sunday morning, no one the wiser. But behind that smile was a lonely heart and the need for a real Jesus. Lance was a searcher, and like the prodigal, his search would take him home again.

As an artist Lance found his home away from home in the pop art of the youth culture. His imagination and intuition were sensitively transmitted through his hands. Lacking the discipline of a commercial artist he did what pleased him, mastering many things without bothering to perfect any. From water colors to oils, from metal sculpture to junk art assemblages, Lance created and expressed himself. His environment was "funky," reflecting the return to the primitive and the natural characteristic of the Woodstock generation.

Then it happened, simply and profoundly. After a Wednesday night Bible study, Lance went home,

knelt by his bed and gave his life to God. Now there was more than the grin. An inner light had been turned on, and like moths to a fire, searchers intuitively were drawn to the light they saw in Lance. Through Lance the artist and now the Christian, the door to pop art was opened for the gospel and for me. Again, my ministry would not be the same.

●

Gary's parents were the faithful Christians who salt the church and thereby preserve it. They periodically gave me reports on their renegade son whom I had known momentarily through a high school ski trip and who then, like so many others, dropped from view. He was interested in things mechanical, especially racing bikes and cars. Might there be some way through these that I could contact him? There wasn't. Gary identified with the great automotive subculture finding its womb in Southern California. Drugs were now heavily lodged in that subculture and in Gary's car club.

Then, one evening as the sun hung over the Pacific, Gary, now in his early twenties, having gone through cars, drugs, and hard rock music, dropped to his knees on a high bluff and surrendered his life to Jesus Christ. The change was immediate and dramatic. Gary had to lead the pack in racing, and this energy and need was now channeled into his faith. His friends were the first to know, and one by one they had to take sides.

The relief and warmth of Gary's mother told me of her son's conversion. Would I call him? I did, and eventually through Gary's friends I entered a

new world: a world where drugs contended for bodies and souls; a world where drugs were not a weekend high, but a center for life; a world with its own language, symbols, art, and music; a world of lawyers, "connections," "busts," "coping" and the O.D.; a world of crime, power, staggering fear and death. Needless to say, my ministry was at another turning point. I could not flee this grim enemy, and with Gary standing with me I crossed that new threshold.

●

Tom grew up in a nominally Roman Catholic family. His youth saw vacillation between studies, sports, gangs, music, and drugs. After saving money from a factory job he moved to Big Bear Lake, high above Los Angeles, where he practiced his music and worked at a ski tow. Then some Christians from Calvary Chapel in Costa Mesa passed through Tom's life. Through them Christ passed into Tom's life, and a few months later in the fall of 1970, Tom and a couple of friends drove a 1919 Nash from Chicago to Los Angeles to evangelize the country with their newfound faith. In the Middle West a pastor invited Tom to remain behind to minister to the youth of Wichita. For Tom this was the call of God, and he began Saturday night meetings of prayer, singing, and sharing in the pastor's church.

Four weeks later I walked in on one hundred people sitting on the floor praising God. Tom sat on a stool in front, long hair, bearded, with a glow on his face and a smile which were instinctively contagious. The songs and the spirit let me know I was in the Christian family. Afterward Tom and I embraced like long lost friends, and I discovered

19

a young Christian of great maturity, wisdom, and sensitivity. Through Tom and many others I later found my way back to Wichita for a city-wide evangelistic effort. Through Tom a new challenge was placed before me: a new generation of Christian leadership without seminary training or ordination was rising up with the Spirit of God upon their lives, the love of God in their hearts, and the Word of God on their lips. What was the church to do with this anointed leadership? Again my ministry was taking a new turn.

This is a personal story of my response to cultural and spiritual crisis and change. Abandoning the security of my academic and ecclesiastical credentials I had to hear the cry of a generation and respond to that cry. In my response I discovered a thousand other responses spanning the West coast and then fanning across the nation. The slick magazines would call it "The Jesus Movement." I see it as a genuine spiritual awakening taking the multiforms of the youth culture and going far beyond that culture. We begin, with Cheryl, on the streets.

2

the streets of hollywood

Cheryl took me to the streets. The summer of 1967 found the hippie world in full swing. I discovered Hollywood Boulevard and the Sunset Strip only blocks from the church building which had served as an effective buffer between myself and the surrounding community. It was a swirling world of bizarre dress and bizarre behavior. "Love" and "peace," ideals that too often only meant sex and drugs, still expressed genuine longings. By their outlandish costumes and freaky hair these "flower children" were not only "putting down" the technological society and social ladder of suburbia, but also crying out to be recognized as real persons, unique individuals. They called each other "beautiful," looking for that inner beauty of which the Bible so often speaks, rather than the status symbols of a manipulated mass society.

I was rightly impressed with the honest, engaging conversations that were possible in the "hip" world. No longer did I have to watch my dress and monitor my words, carefully looking for the opportunity to speak of Christ, as I had done in the fraternities and sororities on the campus. Here all was wide open. My first conversation with Cheryl and her roommate Michelle covered everything from God, sex, parents, the Bible, drugs, church, and the future in rapid-fire conversation. Was I a virgin? (I was.) Had I done drugs? (I hadn't.) Was Christ real to me? (He was.) Elements of this conversation were repeated again and again that summer. My defenses began to go. I was either honest or out. There were no alternatives.

God used Cheryl to teach me many things in the great process of setting me free. One week after I met her she came again to church, rushed across the patio, threw her arms around me and gave me a big kiss. For a young, unmarried minister who had avoided any hint of scandal, I was stunned. I felt as if my head were turning 360 degrees looking for the church's elders, while every muscle in my body froze. Later in reflection on this incident I realized that Cheryl was only being her street self. I further realized that while I talked about Christian freedom, Cheryl actually was much more free than I. It was a new world indeed that I was entering.

I began to listen to that world. I saw its notorious

underground papers, felt its anarchic and escapist spirit, heard the false promises of its hallucinogenic drugs, and saw the influx of Eastern religion offer a new spirituality to Western minds fed up with pragmatism and materialism. I reeled under its biting criticism of racism and war. I blushed at the silence of the church and fought the temptation to become defensive. My deepest listening came at the point of its music. Here I began to feel the full weight of the cultural revolution, and here I found a great secret: music is the key to this generation because music is the one place in the mass media where kids editorialize to kids.

If I may become Freudian for a moment, with Elvis Presley in the middle '50s the American sex symbol shifted from the quarterback to the musician. Prior to Presley the young male could act out his sexuality indirectly only by throwing the touchdown pass and leaving victoriously with the blond cheerleader on Friday night. Now with "Elvis the Pelvis," the musician could act out his sexuality with guitar in hand in a way which was unheard of even in Sinatra's day. Thus the new long hair brought in by the Beatles was anything but effeminate to their young admirers.

More than this, with the revival of folk music in the later '50s and the civil rights struggle, message music became "in," and the music counted. Dylan emerged as the young hero-king and his hit, "Blowin' in the Wind," not only stopped the Newport Folk Festival but also became the marching song of an idealistic generation organizing for change.

If Dylan fed the minds of the young, the Beatles fed

their feelings. With rock music, electric guitars, and amps a total atmosphere was created demanding full participation. This easily became wed to drugs for those seeking an environmental alternative to the middle-American mass culture. Thus we got hard and acid rock.

It is to the musicians, then, that we must look to understand the form and content of the youth culture. The musicians are its prophets, priests, and kings. As prophets they criticize. As priests they offer communion. As kings they conquer and rule. At Woodstock we were treated to the spectacle of a twentieth century pilgrimage to Jerusalem, the Holy City, where the priests made their musical sacrifices on the high altar before an awed congregation. If then the musicians offer the form of the youth culture, what about content? As I listened to their music, a new—yet old—value system began to emerge through the lyrics. Simple words regained their force: hope, love, truth, peace. We will look briefly at them.

Dotson Rader, ex-SDS leader and son of evangelist Paul Rader, describes his friends as "a generation of believers looking for a cause." This has led to many commitments to many causes offering hope, from the Communist party to Ralph Nader to the Sierra Club. Some high points of this optimism about the future were the civil rights campaign to register voters in the South, the "children's crusade" on behalf of Eugene McCarthy, and the moritorium marches to end the Vietnam War. Hope, being a largely undefined ideal, was maintained through many causes and limited successes. But hope there was, bringing a commitment to the future, however utopian, rather than a mere drop-out from the present.

Love, also a largely undefined ideal, focused the quest for community, the recovery of the personal, the need for acceptance and warm human relationships. It might mean as little as looking for "good vibes," or free sex, or as much as the sacrifice of one's life.

The longing for love bore within it the rejection of our performance-oriented culture, where acceptance is qualified, starting at home: "Yes, I love you, but go clean up your room"; or "Yes, I love you, but get a haircut." The longing for love stood against the values of our technological society, which absolutized reason, order, and function over the individual. The longing for love stood against the values of our intellectual community, which so often played "mind games" as a defense against becoming personal and really seeking the truth.

Once again, Woodstock symbolized the return to natural simplicity and true community in the quest for love, uninhibited by machines, steel, glass, and concrete. As the song "Woodstock" of Crosby, Stills, Nash, and Young put it, "We've got to get ourselves back to the garden," the cry of each Adam and Eve east of Eden.

Also truth became important to this generation. Look beyond the image; listen beyond the propaganda. There are "beautiful people" beyond the "plastic society." Find the inner beauty which is the real truth. The jump into subjectivity led to a new definition of absolutes, no longer measured by reason, but now by experience. As the rock hero Jimi Hendrix wrote, "There is no good or bad. There are only good experiences and bad experiences." Whether this subjectivism had any stability was doubtful, but the demand for experience and experiential confirmation could not be avoided. No longer could concepts be tested by more concepts. Now they must be tested by experience. Out of confrontation the truth would emerge, it was hoped, but truth *was* demanded, regardless of the form it took.

Peace as an ideal of non-violence reentered our culture from Jesus' Sermon on the Mount, through Gandhi and Martin Luther King. Not only the race struggle but also the Vietnam war cried out for peace. The ideal of non-violence was reinforced by the turn to Eastern religion led especially by George Harrison and John Lennon of the Beatles. This quest for peace became reinforced again by drug use, which promised peace now, at least for the individual. Timothy Leary wrote, "Reason is a tissue thin artifact easily destroyed by a slight alteration in the body's biochemistry." Once reason was gone, peace could be achieved, even if it were only a euphoric fog or hallucinogenic high.

These, then, were some of the basic values articulated by the musicians to this generation. It is true that songs were written advocating virtually everything. It is also true, paradoxically, that big business paid the bills through advertising to keep on the air a value system quite contrary to adult society. But it is also true that serious questions were raised through these songs that demanded a response from the gospel.

So one Sunday evening in the fall of 1967 Bob, my musician friend, and I stepped on the platform at Hollywood Presbyterian Church with a Dylan songbook. Bob sang Dylan's music to punctuate my sermon with his questions while the congregation followed along on a song sheet and I gave an answering commentary.

Needless to say it was a controversial evening. It forced the congregation that night to face the music and the longings of the youth culture. It forced people to see that Jesus Christ authentically answers these longings. But learning to listen in order to understand is difficult, and there was a reaction. Some felt we had desecrated the "Temple of the Lord" by bringing in secular music. Some felt we were endorsing Dylan's life-style by using his music. I responded as best I could. I reminded people that when we quoted Shakespeare and Plato from the pulpit we were not endorsing their theology or their ethics. I pointed out that the poet-prophets in our culture had much to say to us, and we to them. Above all I asserted that the purpose of our service was to draw the outside within range of the gospel; we had other services to lift the hearts of the saints to God. I knew of nowhere in the Bible where God expected people to worship him before they knew him.

As we won the argument and went on, the breakthrough to the culture outside had begun. By spring we had to open our balcony on Sunday evening for these monthly services, destroying not only the myth of Ed Sullivan's television omnipotence, but also the myth that people won't come off the streets into the church. Over 1200 of the greatest conglomeration of humanity I had ever seen gathered in April for a service on "Bob Dylan and Jesus Christ." We had made our point and were now ready for a more sustained effort in reaching the youth culture around us. It was then that Lance, my artist friend, became crucial in our effort, for from Lance was to come The Salt Company Coffee House.

3

the
salt
company

Tens of thousands of teen-agers flood Hollywood each weekend. The traffic backs up the freeway halfway to the Civic Center as aimless drivers come to "cruise the Boulevard" and parade themselves and their cars. The city still has attraction in its declining years. Theaters line the streets, mixed now with topless bars and pornographic book stores revealing the state of its fall—a modern Corinth.

Most of these roaming youth will never enter a church on Sunday. They view it as a social club rather than as a center of spiritual power. Many have rejected a "junior high Jesus," failing to see the commanding Christ of maturity. Furthermore, many feel that with their dress and looks they would be quickly frozen out. To these youth we are called. As my friend Dick Langford puts it, "Nowhere in the New Testament is the world commanded to come into the church and be saved. Everywhere in the New Testament is the church commanded to go into the world with the message of salvation."

But how shall we go? Our clue comes from the Apostle Paul who became all things to all men in order to win some. The form of our approach must have a contemporary cultural identification, while the content must remain unchanging.

Our first step was to build the Salt Company Coffee House in the summer of 1968. The name "Salt Company" was thought up by Lance, taken from Jesus' word, "Ye are the salt of the earth." "Company" means a body of committed people called to be salt—to flavor and preserve the world.

The Salt Company was designed to be a place for the musical communication of the gospel in an atmosphere which emphasized relational evangelism. It was to become a bridge to the non-Christian world. We described it to our congregation as an "evangelistic facility." Too often we exhort Christians to "witness" without showing them how, which creates only guilt and apathy. The Salt Company was a place where Christian kids from all over could bring their friends, to expose them to the gospel in a contemporary and natural way. At the same time, many came in on their own initiative off Hollywood Boulevard and the Sunset Strip.

Lance set to work in the spring to design the facility. We settled on the upstairs of a two-storey apartment building owned by the church. It was old and crumbly and offered the "funky," non-institutional atmosphere which we were looking for. Lance decided on the decor. It was a cross between Disneyland's Main Street and Knott's Berry Farm. The furniture was country-western, late Victorian-Salvation Army. Lance designed a main entertainment room seating 100, finished in old wood from a dismantled barn. Tacked onto the walls were samples of Lance's junk art. A small stage, a lighting and sound system, and round conversation tables completed the room.

Along with an office and a prayer room, Lance built a snack bar with swinging doors looking like an old Western saloon, and a recreation room with pool and ping pong tables in the spirit of the San Francisco's Gay '90s.

Throughout the building an atmosphere of warmth was created as a context for communicating the gospel. This was the meaning of our recreation room—a place where people could play together and relate casually. This was also the meaning of our entertainment area—tables where people could see each other, where they could relax and chat. We avoided the sterile asphalt tile, metal folding chairs, and fluorescent tubing of institutional church life. We also avoided the black lights and psychedelic posters of the drug world. We were here to love people to Jesus, and the building was to help, not hinder that effort.

31

The leadership of the church agreed with our plans and loaned us the $12,000 necessary to launch the operation. The monthly overhead was carried by charging a donation on the weekends for two-act live musical shows. In the first year we received enough money in donations and reserves from our door receipts to pay back our debt. Over 10,000 kids passed through on the weekends to see the programs. Many more came in and out during the week.

Now we had the place, but we needed music. What Dylan did for the youth culture, we could do for the gospel. The same type of music which turned kids on to drugs could be used to turn them on to Christ. Bob Marlowe with his guitar stepped in and David Covington, Pam and Tim Van Valin, Jean Zentmyer, and Brian Hahn joined him to form the Salt Company musical group. Using folk rock music, acoustical guitars, and electric bass, they began to sing the gospel, soon composing their own songs. They became the leading Christian group on the coast and held concerts on college and high school campuses where a minister could never go and preach. Here much seed was sown which would later blossom into the "Jesus Movement."

Our primary evangelistic intention was soon being realized. Conversations would go late into the night. Decisions for Christ were made. A small group of Christians moved near the church to be available at all hours. Lance became our director while Cheryl became our hostess, knowing intuitively what was going on with people off the streets.

Now a body of new believers was forming, many with no previous church connection. We decided to baptize them, but the regular Presbyterian coat-and-tie sprinkling on Sunday morning had little appeal. So off we went on a Sunday afternoon to Hansen Dam to immerse these new Christians. It was natural and primitive and right. As they went down into the water, expressing their dying to the old life and rising to the new, witnessing before the world rather than simply the church, we all had the sense that the gospel was going to go back on the streets again, as it had in the first century.

The Salt Company also gave us an added bonus we did not expect. The "hip" Christians who were later to be identified with the "Jesus Movement" were drawn to us as they would never have been to the institutional church. They felt at home with Lance's warm personality and off-beat life-style. Bob Engle from Long Beach, the "repent or perish" messenger of the Sunset Strip with painted warnings on his van, came, as did Dan Poly, ex-doper from Hacienda Heights, who now ran a Christian commune and commanded a following in the hundreds. Larry Norman, rock musician, now converted to Christ, heard "The Agape," a hard rock Christian group, play songs about Jesus. This convinced Larry that he could use his rock music to communicate the gospel, and later he was to release a Christian album through Capitol Records called "Upon this Rock" and become a leader in the music of the "Jesus Movement." Here then was a melting pot for these emerging Christians to meet and connect with each other. For many the Salt Company became home and a springboard to further ministry.

The Salt Company was a bridge, but we were still asking people to walk over it to come to us, rather than going over it to them. By the next summer we were ready to go over it ourselves. Twenty-five of us took the summer, raised a budget to meet our needs, and hit the beaches with our music and our message.

Living together around the church we would study and pray in the early morning and then get on a big yellow bus to go to the beach. There we set up a portable stage and sound system and then circulated about inviting the local sun-worshippers to a free concert at noon. The Salt Company group or Larry Norman would play for 40 minutes, and a short gospel message and testimony would be given to the several hundred gathered about. One little girl thanked us for coming because she liked music but couldn't afford the big secular concerts. It seemed appropriate to me that Christians should come on to the beach singing.

At Sorrento Beach, near Santa Monica, the young teen-agers gather to eye each other and do their drugs. One day early in the summer Steve Skinner, who was to enter high school in the fall, heard the music and stopped to talk. That day Steve gave his life to Christ on the beach, where six weeks later he was to drown. The change in Steve's life immediately influenced his friends and family. His mother Evelyn has expressed it in her own words:

At the end of the school year last June Steve left home for about two weeks—a result of poor grades, plus a lack of communication and agreement with his parents about his choice

of friends, mode of dress, length of hair, and many other subjects. The so called generation gap was very apparent at this time in our lives. Upon Steve's return, we started twice-weekly sessions with a psychologist well-known for his work with adolescents. We learned much from these meetings—of experiments with drugs, a feeling of discontent, a search for something. During the fourth session, I was astounded to hear from our shy, quiet son that he would no longer need these sessions because his life had completely changed. When the doctor questioned him further, Steve said, "Yesterday at the beach I accepted Jesus Christ as my personal Savior and I'm happy." After more conversation, the doctor agreed with Steve that further sessions would be superfluous, that he had indeed turned a corner.

I learned that on the particular day Steve referred to, he had been attracted by a quartet of young people at the beach who played guitars and sang beautifully. Their songs were of Jesus. After a large crowd gathered to hear the music, several young men and women then spoke about Jesus and how he could change their lives. They subsequently spent more time talking individually to any who were interested. Steve talked at some length with Pete Ross, the beach team captain, and then knelt in prayer on the sand with him to accept Christ into his life. He was given a simplified New Testament to begin studying.

Steve was attending summer school to make up a failing grade. Following his experience with

Christ at the beach, each day right after school he would head for the beach and talk to as many of his friends and acquaintances as he saw about Jesus and the Bible, which he studied daily. This in itself was surprising to me since Steve had always disliked reading of any kind.

My husband and I had planned to take a fishing-camping vacation in the mountains after summer school ended, and Steve, his seventeen-year-old sister, and four other teen-agers were going along for the fun. We planned to leave on a Sunday, and on the previous Wednesday morning Steve asked me if he could stay late at the beach to do some body-surfing and to watch the sunset. I said yes to his request, and he promised to be home by eight o'clock p.m. By midnight, however, it became apparent he was not coming home for the night. For the first time in my life I wasn't worried; I told a close friend that wherever he was, the Lord was with him. I thought probably he had decided to spend the night with a friend and neglected to call.

Thursday and Friday came and went, and although I called many of Steve's friends, no one had seen him since Wednesday. Saturday my husband and I worked all day loading the trailer with enough food and supplies for six teenagers and ourselves for our ten-day stay in the mountains. We were confident that Steve would return home by Sunday morning to go with us on our long-planned vacation. At eight o'clock p.m. my husband and I were just leav-

ing the house to have a quick dinner at a neighborhood restaurant when we heard the squeal
of brakes and hurrying up the drive came Don
Williams and Pete Ross saying they had to talk
to us.

How do you tell parents that their only son
is dead? I realized later what an ordeal it was
for these two young men who had come to
know and love Steve so dearly.

Thus began the most anguish-filled night of
my life, as they gently told us that Steve had
possibly drowned and that we were to ac-
company them downtown to the morgue to
identify a body known only as John Doe. I
remember that my knees buckled for a moment
as I said, "I don't believe this is happening."
I remember saying then, much more from des-
perate hope than from inner faith, "If this is
true, the Lord will give me the strength."

It was indeed the body of our son which had
washed upon the beach Thursday morning.
When Don came to see us the next day, he
told us of the miracle which had taken place
the day before. He had been at the beach quite
by chance and said he had felt led to stop by
a particular beach club to talk to a friend of
his. Don hadn't seen him for some time, and
they chatted for about fifteen minutes. Just as
Don was about to leave, his friend said. "By
the way, we had a harrowing experience here
on Thursday morning." He told of seeing the
body of a young boy washing in on the beach
and calling the police who took the body to

the morgue, for, of course, there was no identification. Don, knowing that Steve had not as
yet returned home, asked for a description of
the boy. Upon hearing it, he immediately found
Pete and they drove to the morgue, after which
they hurried to our house in one of the many
outlying suburbs to break the sad news. Other-
wise, our son would have been buried as 'John
Doe' without our ever knowing what had happened.

After Pete and Don left our house that Saturday evening, I made a few phone calls and
finally went to bed a little after midnight. I
sat in the dark alone, numb with shock, and
finally went to sleep around two-thirty. I awoke
at four o'clock a.m. and was so engulfed in
grief and disbelief I felt as though I were gasp-
ing for air. I knew only that I had to walk. I
slipped on a pair of shoes, pulled a coat over
my nightgown, and quietly let myself out of
the house. I walked for many miles, not knowing or caring where, weeping and crying out
to God for help.

Some hours later I became dimly aware that
the sky was beginning to pale, and I remem-
bered how our son had loved to watch the
sunrise. From somewhere deep inside me I
heard myself saying, "I'll watch this sunrise
with you, Stevie." I have never seen a more
beautiful sight. As the sky turned glorious
colors of pinks and golds and the sun rose
above the soft white cloud formations, a sense
of peace came over me as I sensed that indeed
the Lord and Steve and I were together sharing

this beauty. It seemed as though I could hear Steve saying to me, "Don't cry, Mom, I'm happy. I'm with my beloved Jesus."

I learned later that on the last day of Steve's life on earth around dinner time he had made a phone call from the beach and had talked to young Patty Ross, Pete's bride of two months. He said to her, "I have just spent the neatest day I've ever had with Jesus, just talking to and being with him all day. I'm going to watch the sunset and do a little body-surfing this evening. I always feel closest to the Lord at the beach."

Apparently later that evening a big wave caught him and took him home to his Lord. How complete and fitting that it was there that Steve first accepted Christ. He began a new life on earth and another one in eternity, both at the beach.

We have received hundreds of cards and letters testifying to the impact of Steve's faith. They have come from young people, parents, people who only saw Steve once, but whose lives were touched in many ways. One mother wrote, "Only Stevie could bring Jimmy to Christ." Another young man wrote, "I only talked with Steve a few times but his new-found life was an inspiration and taught me much."

We thank God we were indeed blessed to have had our son with us for his 15 years. I know too that without God we would never have been able to accept this loss and grow in faith. The Lord has shown us many miracles of his grace and love and, most of all, the great power of what perfect faith in one young boy accomplished in changing the lives of so many from empty searching to purposeful living, in preparation for that wonderful life in eternity.

We had gone to the beaches to take Christ to those who would not come to us and they, like Steve, had brought Christ to us in a new way. It was a decisive move; we were in the community and there was no retreat. The ministry begun through Steve continues in North Hollywood two years later.

Other ways of moving the gospel to the world began to emerge. During that summer of '69 Duane Peterson, a ventriloquist-entertainer, walked into my office with the first edition of his underground Christian newspaper, *The Hollywood Free Paper.* I was excited that Duane had done something to help get the gospel on the streets and immediately offered our help. Lance went to work giving a new layout, masthead, and cartoons to Duane's first attempt. I contributed some articles, and we set up distribution in the Salt Company. At a Salt Company gospel-rock concert later at the Pasadena Civic Auditorium we took a special offering to help Duane. Duane's paper was to become the leading underground Christian paper appealing to the younger teen-agers and ex-dopers finding Jesus, and serving as a communications organ for the "Jesus Movement."

That fall also Lance came to me with a new Christian symbol. It was a take-off on the Harvard Uni-

versity strike symbol which had a red clenched fist and the word "Strike" stenciled beneath. Lance had one finger now pointing to heaven with a small cross above it and stenciled beneath, the slogan "One Way." This was to travel nation-wide as the symbol of the "Jesus Movement."

1969 was a year of marches. Not only was the commercialized Santa Claus Lane parade held on Hollywood Boulevard, but the Gay Liberation Front demonstrated there as well. We felt it was time for Christians to become more visible, so, at Christmas time we went down to the Boulevard, 5,000 strong with banners and posters proclaiming our faith. Jack Sparks of the Christian World Liberation Front in Berkeley, Hal Lindsey, author of *The Late Great Planet Earth,* Bob Kraning, youth evangelist, Ed Hill, black leader, and I shared the platform on the football field at Hollywood High School with Larry Norman and the Salt Company and a black choir. The police expressed amazement at the cooperation and love felt that day. At Easter time 8,000 of us marched to the south end of the City Hall to proclaim to Los Angeles that Jesus had risen from the dead. Similar marches by then were being held up and down the West coast.

In new and experimental ways we were struggling back to those streets from which Cheryl had come, it seemed, so long ago. But it was one thing to march on Hollywood Boulevard or invite people to the Salt Company from the Boulevard, and another to go there to stay. God was not through with us yet; the fulfillment of our discipleship was still ahead, brought about, paradoxically, by the national catastrophe of drug abuse.

4

this
grim
enemy

"Mark is shooting heroin," Gary said, and I panicked. My memory flashed on a three-year relationship with an old-line drug addict from the jazz world, Dan Howe, which had ended with his funeral.

After Gary's conversion several of his friends had met Christ, many of them more than experimenters in the drug world. Tim was one of these new Christians, once a burly high school football player and now an engineering student at UCLA. Mark, his younger brother, had dropped out of UCLA because of his drug abuse and was living at home.

Mark's history, like so many, was one of continual hassle with the law, in and out of jail and lawyers' offices. Mark was able to pay for his freedom, and he did, but the point of no return was near. In despair his parents had given him up for dead. Mark had gone through all the drugs, becoming an expert by experience. He had dropped acid (used LSD) over 500 times. His best experience was with reds (barbiturates, or sleeping pills). When I first met Mark he was taking 11 pills a day to maintain his habit, and when he really wanted to feel good he went up to 16.

Mark's turning to heroin prompted my question to Gary, "When do we go to see him?" It was a Saturday, and we called to see if he was home. He was, and we went.

I couldn't think of any casual way to walk into the bedroom of a young drug addict whom I had never met. My experience said, "Be honest." So in we went, and I said, "Hi, Mark, we've come to share with you the life we have found in Jesus." This launched us into three hours of discussion in which Gary and I related our testimonies and the basic Christian good news. Most of the time Mark listened, although obviously sedated by his barbiturates, and asked a few questions. During the time there, several of Mark's doper friends showed up and joined the discussion, including one of the chief pushers in Westchester where he lived. Mark's mother, not knowing me, passed the room glaring. Apparently she felt we were there to deal in drugs.

This was the beginning of several arduous months.

We had a relationship with Mark through his Christian brother Tim, which allowed us to launch a Bible study in his living room. We invited several old friends of Gary's and Tim's, making sure that Mark was warmly included. He did his best to avoid us and to lose himself in his girlfriend and drugs while we were there. One evening he waited outside several hours so he wouldn't have to face us.

An ex-heroin addict named John joined us for our study, and one night he was able to share with Mark his conversion experience in jail. Mark listened. Here was a man who had been where he had been and found Christ. A telling point was made.

A few weeks later the crisis came. Mark had a falling out with his old doper friends, and had to leave his home. To whom could he turn in this emergency? Gary, his Christian friend was there, and we moved Mark to John's apartment in Hollywood. After Mark accepted Christ into his life the real battle began. The issue was clear: would Mark give all to Jesus, or try to maintain himself with both drugs and Christ? We talked seriously one Sunday after church, and I remember telling Mark that he could not serve two masters, "both God and Mammon."

Mark went that afternoon with Gary and me to my apartment nearby. We were at an impasse. Having accepted Christ, Mark was still using barbiturates. I feared now that he would simply want to go back home and give up Christ. The conversation was moving that way. Suddenly Mark said to Gary, "Let's go outside." I remained praying feverishly, and they returned triumphantly. Mark had given a bag of 70 pills to Gary to throw down the drain. Again and again with Mark I was to experience miracles at the impasse. God was pounding into me a total reliance upon himself, which I would only accept when my back was against the wall.

What should we do now? We decided to spend a few days at a mountain cabin to "cool off," and after picking up another friend, Rick, we left immediately. That night Mark slept little, but his spirits were good. I returned home early the next day for a speaking engagement and decided to visit Mrs. Klein in the probation department, who had advised me on drug problems in the past. When I told her that Mark had "put down" barbiturates, she replied that we must hospitalize him at once. He could not just stop taking these chemicals on his own without the severe danger of a deadly seizure. I raced back to the cabin, fearing what I might find.

I burst in upon a tranquil scene and was greatly relieved. Nevertheless, we decided to leave after dinner and get Mark to a hospital. I lay down for a rest only to be called back to reality by frantic voices, "Mark's on the floor." Flying into the living room, I found Mark prone, every muscle in his body contracted, his breathing stopped, his eyes rolled back and his flushed face turning ashen. I acted instinctively, forcing my index finger between his clenched teeth and with Rick joining me, we pulled with all our might while Gary called the rescue squad.

The pain of Mark's teeth cutting into my finger

only made me pull harder. Finally, the teeth separated and a suck of air went through them into his lungs. It was one of the most beautiful sounds I have ever heard. The color returned to Mark's face, his eyes opened, and when the rescue squad arrived, he was fully conscious. I thanked God for the timely warning of Mrs. Klein.

After ten days of detoxification at Los Angeles County Hospital, Mark returned home to Westchester—against my better judgment. Immediately the old doper friends came around like sea gulls to a fishing boat. I made daily trips to see Mark. I had fought this far; I wasn't about to give up now.

Within a week Mark had taken his first pill again. With Gary's help I was able to spot the symptoms. Over coffee I told Mark that I loved him, cared about him, would do anything for him, and that I knew he wasn't making it at home. He admitted that it was true and asked in desperation what we could do. "Let's live together," I proposed. Thus, Mark and Gary and I moved in together that same day. Our love had to act at some cost to our "private life."

Within a month we had lived in three different places while looking for a house. A realtor in our church helped us, and an old two-story antique, destined to be removed for commercial development, became available on Virgil Street in Los Angeles. We moved in.

I had now learned three important things in dealing with the drug problem. The first was the value of fellow Christians like Gary and John who had

51

already been through it. They speak with a knowledge and integrity from experience which I do not have. They formed a small Christian community which could operate with love and sensitivity and sheer physical support which I could not produce alone. The second, of course, was the power of Jesus Christ to change lives, to meet the deep longings which drugs could only temporarily fill, at best. This power was not abstract and was released again and again by simple prayer. The third was the necessity for a new living environment for true and lasting rehabilitation. We had to live together. Only then could the kind of support be given day by day to help Mark stabilize. Being under the same roof we could keep the old friends away and pray and share together to help Mark in his new life in Christ. I hadn't planned on going into the housing business or starting a Christian commune, but God had put me there. I quickly was to learn a fourth thing—the importance of a job.

Mark needed to restructure his life. He needed to stop living off society. Through Christ he needed to gain a new self-image made practical by the dignity of work and self-support. He needed to have his time used up. He needed to get physically tired. All of this a job would provide, but how could we find a job? Mark could not drive; his license was suspended. Many jobs would mean renewed contacts with drug abuse, and this negative environment was a threat to Mark's rehabilitation. Furthermore, the economy made jobs scarce, and Mark was not only unskilled but non-competitive because of the long dissipation of his body. These problems were answered finally when my father gave Mark a job on a construction project where the superintendent, a Christian, knew of his problems. The immediate need was met, but the question of jobs remained, especially if we were really going to be serious about drug rehabilitation.

Our new house prospered. Here was the crucible for the Christian life. We were living together, and our roommates were of God's choosing, not ours. Stan came with a drug problem, John with a nervous breakdown, and then there was Devon whose life became instrumental for many things God had yet to show us.

Devon came from Wichita. His father, a successful psychologist and elder in his Presbyterian church, contacted me through relatives in California. Would I come to Wichita to advise his church on their drug abuse problem, which had become personal, trapping both of his older sons? That is how I met Devon at Prairie View Psychiatric Hospital outside of Wichita on my first visit. He was a tall, good looking boy of 19 with long hair and a wide smile. Devon and I talked for a couple of hours. He knew I was there as a minister because of his father's request, but this did not make him defensive. I had an opportunity to share my personal experience of Christ and his meaning for my life. In the course of our conversation I told Devon Jesus' parable of the prodigal son. When I described how the father embraced and kissed his son upon his return home Devon exclaimed, "Gosh, I wish my dad would do that to me."

Devon had lived in a performance-oriented community and family. Good marks, good behavior, good appearance were important as signs of success for himself and his parents. Devon had them all, yet he was unhappy. As he expressed it to me, "At age 17 I left home for the first time to go to Kansas University. During this year I studied psychology and history. I was a gymnast on the varsity squad and vice-president of my fraternity pledge class. I was also about a year into using drugs at this time. My year at school proved quite unfruitful. What I thought would be the start of a road to happiness, a road to finding myself and where I was going in this society, didn't turn out that way because of my lack of motivation and direction. I had no purpose in life; I was very insecure about myself and what I was doing." So Devon and several others got more deeply into drugs and dropped out. His parents intervened, and he ended up in the psychiatric hospital where I visited him.

While in Wichita, I made another trip on my own to see Devon, to let him know I wanted to be with him and cared about him as a person. Then I returned to California. During the early spring I went to speak in Minnesota and routed myself through Wichita to see Devon. I wanted him to know that my love for him was not merely a professional responsibility.

In I dropped to find Devon's life at a dead end. He had left the hospital while continuing therapy, gone to school again briefly and was now working in a factory, living with a couple of friends in a small town outside of Wichita. Where he was living, people would try to run him off the road when bike riding because of his long hair. I took him to dinner and laid my proposal on him, "Come to California and live with me." (By this time our house with Mark was going.) The only thing I asked Devon to do was to be open to the possibility of Christ for his life if he came. He promised to think it over. I would be near Wichita in a month and would call him and bring him to California if this was his decision. It was; he came. Later Devon confessed that he wore long-sleeved shirts on the trip so that I would not see the needle marks on his arms from shooting "speed" (a stimulant which speeds up the system and is very lethal).

Devon moved into our little community and again our lives and our faith were on the line. Devon asked serious questions; the change in Mark's life impressed him. As with Gary and John to Mark, so with Mark to Devon; he had been where Devon was. Devon watched us read the Bible and pray; he also watched us live normal lives with our hassles. Then on a Friday night as we prayed together in John's apartment, Devon joined our prayers for the first time and simply asked Christ to take his life. That was it. We all looked up in wonder. Devon is a quiet, strong person, and his conversion was in character.

Devon immediately wanted to bring to California Mary Lee, his non-Christian girlfriend, whom he had met in the hospital. With much fear and trembling we agreed. Mary Lee had been heavy into drugs, on the streets, and was an acute schizophrenic. She came, and her first words off the plane were, "Devon, whatever has got into you?" In a matter of weeks it got into Mary Lee too, and she accepted Christ. Mary Lee's schizophrenia has never recurred.

55

Devon's conversion was deeply satisfying to me not only for his sake but also because of the risk of faith in bringing him to California and my responsibility to his family. He relates his change in this way:

Since accepting Christ into my life I've been able to take a good look at myself, I've been able to take a good look at what the Bible has to say about me and the world, about my other brothers and sisters in Christ, and to see that the Bible is very relevant to my total life. It covers everything that I really need to know, and what I can't read about I can pray about. I can ask God for answers now. He's promised to fulfill me, and that's what he's doing. Jesus Christ has come to meet me as a human being right where I am, not asking anything of me, except to let me love him and let him love me. This is the power Christ has to offer, love is the major changing force in my life.

My life has been radically changed. Changes that I've been seeking for a long time are now occurring in my life, changes that I've tried to do myself are now being realized. These changes are just given to me by God.

In many conversations with Devon one word keeps surfacing: "hope." Devon now has hope for the future, for himself and those whom he meets, regardless of how lost they are.

What had worked for Mark had worked for Devon: a brotherhood of friends who had been where he was; a new environment; people living the reality of Christ through the totality of their lives, not simply Sunday religion.

It was the spring of 1970, and Mark's drug abuse had opened new doors for changing lives. We had a house with plenty of room. Outside were hurting, lonely people. Cheryl's streets were calling again. Now was the time for getting onto those streets to stay. So we gathered a body of students to reinforce our present core, rented a house across the street for the girls, and entered the summer with our door and hearts open. As Gary put it, "When the Lord started sending us couches we knew the 'crashers' weren't far behind." For hundreds of transient seekers "Virgil House" would become an oasis in the desert of crash pads dotted across the nation. Here was warmth and cleanliness. Here was food and a shower. Here was Christ.

5

the christian commune

When you hit the streets to say to people, "God loves you," and they reply, "I'm hungry, I need a place to crash," what do you do? To use the colloquial: you put up or shut up. I never want to verbalize the gospel and awaken hopes that I am not willing to follow through with and try to fulfill. Jesus is the Good Samaritan who doesn't pass by on the other side, but who meets human need where he finds it. In our churches with their vast buildings and bureaucracies, we have too often been "Jesus Christ Incorporated," to use Kierkegaard's phrase. But Jesus doesn't pass by as we do, and in not stopping, we have really missed him. At Virgil House we rediscovered the Good Samaritan.

When summer came, we hit the streets. Jeff, a seminary student, joined our effort and lent his leadership. He combined the intelligent mind, warm heart, and easy communication we needed. Gary, Mark, and Devon brought their pasts and present to bear on the needs flooding through the house, aided by several others, including Lil, who had worked with teen-age girls professionally for several years. Three who represent so many others especially stand out in my mind from that summer: Verne, Bernard, and Jon.

Almost before we were formally launched, Verne walked through our door, and in him God brought us a special gift.

Verne came from Colorado and was a professional musician. Rebelling against a strict Mormon home, he hit the streets with his guitar and went from bar to bar entertaining with an excellent voice, sensitive poetic spirit, and glowing personality to hide the deep fear, loneliness, and guilt inside. Verne went to the Orient on a U.S.O. tour. He made money and spent money, often leaving unpaid debts and broken relationships behind. Drugs found Verne early, and slowly his life became mostly, as he put it, "getting up, getting loaded, and spending the day nodding out."

While Verne was in Boulder, Colorado, in the spring of 1970, a house was raided by the police, and Verne's guitar filled with drugs was confiscated, although he was not present at the time. Since he was on probation, Verne panicked and fled to San Francisco. There he began to hitchhike south and in Big Sur was picked up by a van filled with dopers.

After the hash-pipe was passed to Verne, he passed it to the long-haired youth beside him who said, "No thanks, I'm a Christian." To continue in Verne's words:

I just handed it on and didn't think too much about it. We came into Los Angeles that night. This Christian guy, Eddie Wyman, asked me if I'd like to find Don Williams, who was a minister friend of his. He told me he'd probably be able to get me some food and a place to sleep. We got to his house on Virgil, and a Christian brother named Devon met me at the door. He put out his hand and said, 'Come on in, man.' He was happy to meet me, and I could see that he thought more of me than most people did. He didn't care what I was, he just "dug" me, and I could feel a difference about him. I went into the house, and they said the place was mine, there was food in the refrigerator, and that I could live there.

That afternoon, after I'd slept for a while, I came downstairs, and some of the brothers there were reading the Bible and were really excited. After sitting for about a half hour and listening to them talk about the love of God, I knew that Jesus was where I wanted to be, so I said, "I want Christ," and Devon asked me if I'd like to pray and I said, "Yes." We all bowed our heads and I said, "Jesus, I want you to come into my life. I want you to forgive me for what I've done, fill me up with the Holy Spirit and just take over my life." I was born again.

This was on a Friday afternoon. By Saturday, Verne the entertainer was in the Salt Company singing songs about Jesus which he composed on the spot. The next day Verne came to church. He relates, "I walked into one of the early morning services, bare-foot with a guitar over my shoulder and grubby clothes on and a middle-aged man walked up to me, held out his hand, and said 'Good morning, brother, come on in.' I knew right away that there is really fellowship in Christ and that people who are Christians really do care for one another." We were making progress.

Verne is an electric personality of immense talent. He has always won his way by his guitar. It was seemingly inevitable for him and us to fall into a trap in his new life.

Since Verne could sing as few others, he easily drew a crowd. Once again my dictum was proven: music is the key to this generation. Through my friend Dave Anderson of Lutheran Youth Alive, Verne traveled and sang all over the Far West. His testimony was real; the light was in his eyes. High school and college campuses were open to him. Tens of thousands heard the message. An album, *Verne Sings,* was released. He got on radio in Salt Lake City and "rapped" about Christ for hours, taking a wide variety of calls on their open line. At a juvenile detention center in Idaho Verne invited any in a roomful of 150 boys to stand to receive Christ. Over half rose to their feet. Here was the itinerant evangelist in the flush of his first experience. No longer was evangelism simply in the hands of the seminary-trained, ordained professional. Verne was in the vanguard of a new breed.

Everywhere he went, the lights went on. He left scores and scores of new lives behind.

This was good and bad. The good is obvious, but the bad was Verne the performer, drawing his crowd through music, covering up the need for deep, honest relationships and the stability and security of knowing that God loved him without his guitar. I rode the spiritual roller coaster with Verne for a year. I asked him to call me collect, night or day, whenever he needed to. He often did. When under pressure in crisis we all tend to revert to the safe old patterns of escape. Verne is no different, and the temptations of the drug world were always at hand.

Through many crises the slow process of maturation was going on. Again, the loving, supporting, forgiving Christian community must be there, on call, and it was. Virgil House was home. Verne knew where he could always come, and the truth of God's unconditional love slowly filtered into his heart, creating a new stability and security. One evening Verne's $550 Martin guitar was stolen by a pusher and sold for $25 to buy drugs. In this deeply symbolic event Verne was freed from his crutch and last "insecure security." As his brother Randy, now too a vibrant believer, was to say: "Our Heavenly Father took the guitar from the musician because the musician loved the guitar more than God."

Now at last Verne was free simply to receive love, and he did. Verne the performer became Verne the person. Later a new guitar was to come to him on the wings of Christian love. Verne has become one

63

of the most gifted Christian communicators of this generation.

Next there was Bernard, a black man from Philadelphia, 27 years of age. He too was a searcher, leaving a close family to look for the missing thing in his life. After being in California for a week, in his words, "I was walking down Hollywood Boulevard just looking around when I ran into a couple of fellows. I asked them for a place to stay, and they invited me over to the Virgil House. I was kind of leery about going with them at first because I saw the pamphlets they had, and one of them spoke to me briefly about Jesus. I was afraid I'd go over there and they'd push religion, and I wasn't really ready for this. At the same time, I was looking for anything so I went with them.

"I got to the house, and the next two or three days Devon spent a lot of time with me sharing things that had happened in his life. The reason for the major change in his life was this person Jesus Christ who could give me fulfillment, who could end this search. There was something that kept drawing me toward what he was saying. He said that all I had to do was ask Christ into my life and ask for forgiveness for my sins. I thought about it quite a bit, 'What could I lose?' I had been through just about everything and nothing clicked, nothing gave me the satisfaction of living or a reason for being here.

"One night we prayed together, and I asked Jesus Christ to come into my life. The next couple of days I knew that something was supposed to change, but I didn't really feel it, and yet at the end of each day as I looked back over the things I had done, the things that were on my mind, a change had really begun. There was concern; I didn't feel as empty; there was also a desire to read the Bible, to find out what this was all about. It's been a rough struggle with lots of ups and downs, a lot of doubt and questioning, but today there's a real joy in knowing that I have Jesus Christ in my life."

Bernard immediately became a quiet leader. He was especially important to me because several years before we had helped black students from the East with their college education by bringing them to California. This program never achieved wide favor in our church and stumbled because of the lack of leadership. Bernard evidenced that leadership which we had not had before. If ex-dopers are best reaching dopers, blacks must reach blacks. The bitter root of segregation, still culturally maintained, will hamper white efforts. Yet I know that Jesus Christ is the answer to rebuilding the negative self-image of blacks caused by white egotism and fear. To show a black person, "You are loved by God, and that's the deepest reason why black is beautiful," is an urgent task of the church. Yet we and the culture have so crippled the blacks that we have destroyed this leadership before it can develop. Bernard is a new breed. Intelligent, wise, warm and Christ-centered, he keeps his cool before racism, understanding it at its sinful core.

Bernard and Devon became the leaders of the Virgil House when fall sent the students back to school. By next summer Bernard was leading his own house in an integrated neighborhood, and recently we baptized ten new black brothers. Men like Bernard are the key to ending racism in America, because Bernard displays in his person how really beautiful God has made black.

The third person that stands out to me from our summer was a homosexual in a special subgroup called "drag queens." An adopted son of a well-to-do Ohio family, Jon had begun his homosexual activity early in life. This had finally led to a dishonorable discharge from the service after a stint in Vietnam.

As a drag queen, Jon was a male homosexual who took the female role, dressing as a woman. His voice, mannerisms, and walk all betrayed this. Jon had drifted to Hollywood, as do so many homosexuals, to find refuge in the large "gay" community. One need not be a moralist to see the tragedy of that world, a tragedy not only of oppression by the straight majority, but a tragedy of fractured relationships caused by the loss of identity and the loneliness of the homosexuals themselves, ever on the hunt, never finding satisfaction.

Jon was looking for help. Being a Presbyterian he found his way to our church and landed in the Salt Company. Jon's approach was defensive; he knew how to use his wit and sarcasm to put everything down, and he did. Behind the front, however, he was crying out. At the Salt Company there was an acceptance which surprised him. Mark especially spent time with Jon and was largely instrumental in Jon's conversion to Christ. An invitation to a Bible study at the Virgil House was quickly accepted, as was an invitation to move in and live with us. Again we were taking a risk. Would Jon's living in a house full of men be the best for him? I was skeptical at first, but we had to get him out of the gay environment and support his desire for a new life.

The community now began to take effect. Jon relates, "I told several people that I had good relationships with about some of my hangups. I had been a homosexual for 13 years, and that's rough to get over. I also used drugs. I could talk to the people that summer about it, but it didn't seem like I was getting anywhere. I went back to homosexual bars several times after I became a Christian, and it was different each time I went. It was like I was the only person in the place who was alive, and I knew it. Lately, I've felt a lot better about myself, accepting my masculine identity. It's still rough sometimes to do that. I know that I couldn't go back to the homosexual life. I can empathize with people in that world because I know what it's like to be a homosexual, and it's not a pleasant life at all, it's just hellish. I'm trying to be a Christian which isn't easy at all. I'm at the point now that I can't imagine being without Jesus Christ. I know there's no other way to live."

Jon's life in the Virgil House was one of agonizingly slow progress. He had a tendency to become emotionally attached to the leadership (the most masculine figures) only to turn that "love" to "hate" when his sexual advances were not accepted. He struggled to be a Christian, to let the gospel give him a new self-image, but he was burdened by a tremendous weight of past history, attitudes, and associations which continually garbled the truth he so desperately wanted to believe. Jon agreed with us that he needed psychological help, and after a period of this, Jon was ready to enter a federally-funded program of rehabilitation for homosexuals. Now the spiritual and psychological could begin to work together. As this is written Jon sends the following letter:

Hi Brother Don,

I'm well, but very, very homesick for the body of believers out there and have prayed on occasions that the Lord might hurry himself a bit in my favor. However, he's apparently in no rush, so I'm praying for patience and practicing longsuffering.

My doctor has started me on a new phase of therapy, and I'm progressing pretty steadily. Praise God! Of course, I do get brought down at times, but the Lord really pulls me out of that. I find myself having to learn to deal with stress situations in new ways. Previously, I'd reverted to the all too familiar ways and means which were invariably gay. This still happens to me, but, Don, the Lord is dealing with that too. Praise Him! The feminine method of defense and retaliation is uncomfortable to me now and practically inoperable.

My doctor has borne witness to the Lord without knowing it. He said, "Out of all my patients in this program, you're the least messed-up." So many of them have to be taught how to sit and talk, walk, what to do, and how to use their hands. He said I didn't need that. Praise

God! But, if you recall, I once would have needed it. The Lord has brought me this far into masculinity, and he'll take me the rest of the way.

This is why the word "hope" is so important to Devon and many other new Christians. We can face ourselves and the future without fear. Christ has opened it for us and takes us through.

The Virgil House grew out of a need and became a ministry. It has now been moved, a year later, to Mariposa Street in Hollywood being, of course, renamed "Mariposa House." A fully staffed girls' house is now also operating across the street. Literally hundreds and hundreds have been ministered to in these facilities. The church is on the streets again—to stay.

Behind these houses support facilities have been created. A non-profit corporation, the Salt Company Mission from Hollywood, now operates a sheltered work shop where simple jobs are provided for youth coming off of drugs. Handicraft, silk-screening posters and bumper stickers, and simple manufacturing aid in their return to society. This arm is sort of a "Goodwill Industry" for the emotionally handicapped. What we needed when Mark put down his drugs, we are creating by selling through our retail art and book store on Hollywood Boulevard, wholesale orders to other book and gift shops, and a mail order business. Much of the art associated with the Jesus Movement is manufactured now in Hollywood. There are "One Way" posters designed by Lance, along with other colorful pop-art Christian posters. Bumper stickers read,

"Honk if you love Jesus," "Read the Bible, it will scare the Hell out of you," "Wise men seek him still," "Find help fast in the Bible pages." Jobs are being created, and the word of Christ is getting out.

Our own underground type newspaper, *The Alternative,* edited by a seminary student, Rich Lange, takes the gospel not only to the streets, but to the campus. Avoiding the often corny Christianized drug language, like "Jesus is the ultimate trip," and "Get high on Jesus," *The Alternative* seeks to be a responsible presentation of the gospel to thinking minds in the youth culture. It is a vast over-simplification to call the Jesus Movement a teeny-bopper fad. It is too diverse for this, simply because the Jesus Movement is an authentic Christian awakening crossing the nation.

Within the life of our church, the Salt Company was the first major structural change. Others were to follow. An early Sunday service was created in the summer of 1970 to minister informally and creatively to those in our congregation who are unmoved by formal worship. Here the congregation often holds hands as it sings and prays. Here members are free to participate with a word of witness or a song. Brightly colored banners created by artist Gloria Wood fly from the front, and on Palm Sunday we all marched around the church with a band to herald Christ's entry into Jerusalem. The spontaneity of the streets is invading our church at many points as things warm up.

In our chapel on Monday nights an informal "underground" worship and evangelistic service was started in the winter. About 150 have met each week to pray and praise God as our emerging young evangelists lead hearty and devotional singing, bring the message and call for decisions, a call regularly heeded.

Thus as we entered 1971 the ministry was maturing. Cheryl called us to the streets and the new culture being created there. Bob interpreted it and showed us how to reach it through his music. Lance gave us a place where youth would come to hear our message. Gary took us to his friends, and we learned the seriousness of ministering to the depths of their needs and the seriousness of our own call to discipleship. Out of that response we were able to go back to the streets to develop ministries to support what God is doing.

Finally we were ready to share what we had learned, and the door again was opening to do just that in Devon's home town of Wichita where Tom Rozof was beginning to work. The Jesus Movement was going nation-wide, and in many ways we were going with it.

6

beyond hollywood

On my first visit to Wichita a Presbyterian pastor, Bob Meyers, heard me say that what Wichita needed was an evangelist who could communicate to its youth in their own language. This pastor later spotted Tom Rozof as he passed through town with his friends on their evangelistic venture. He promptly asked Tom to stay, which Tom did. This was unknown to me as I flew toward Wichita to hold a week of teaching and evangelistic services in Grace Presbyterian Church, from which Devon had come.

Upon my arrival with Devon, a high school boy asked if we cared to attend a Christian meeting that night. We did, and to our amazement and joy we walked into Tom's warm meeting at Faith Presbyterian Church.

When we came, Tom had been there for four weeks. After being asked to stay in Wichita, he moved into the pastor's house, met with the ruling body of the church, and an outreach program to be led by Tom was approved. Although no salary was given, a benevolence fund was established so that interested people could donate to what they saw. The first Saturday night 25 people came. Now there were 100 present, sitting on the floor of the sanctuary from which the folding chairs had been removed.

I asked Tom to sing and share his faith at the meetings we were to hold across town. He was glad to join us.

Before I rose to speak to a capacity crowd the next night, Tom, seated on a stool, sang several contemporary songs about Jesus and shared his own faith. Instead of going to the pulpit, I then instinctively sat on Tom's stool and preached conversationally. The warmth and informality of Tom carried over to my expression, and the personalness and love of the gospel came through aided by this new form of speaking. When our meetings ended on Wednesday night with an overflow crowd, over 60 had come forward at the invitation to confess their faith in Christ. Next Saturday the attendance at Tom's meeting was to double to 200.

Later Devon's dad, Jim, asked, "Where do we go from here?" I suggested that we return to Wichita for a city-wide effort, bringing the Salt Company musical group and a team with us. The wheels began to turn immediately through the Wichita Council on Drug Abuse founded by Jim. Soon a committee of laymen was formed representing a real cross-section of the city's concerned leadership. The downtown civic center, Century II, was secured for five nights of gospel-rock concerts and open evangelistic meetings to be called "Five Days in June."

Meanwhile, in California we gathered a team together. I purposely wanted it as diverse as possible so that no one could say, "Oh yes, the 'Jesus Movement,' I wonder what the kids will get into next?" So, along with Devon, Verne, Gary and the Salt Company musical group, we took John Block, first string forward for the (then) San Diego Rockets of the National Basketball Association, Peter Frankovich of Columbia Pictures in Hollywood, Dave Anderson of Lutheran Youth Alive, musicians Dennis and Danny Agajanian, a young lawyer, a dentist, and several others.

After caravaning to Wichita we all moved into a duplex to live together for a week. From there we fanned out to speak before civic groups, churches, groups of pastors, and to use a massive amount of radio and TV time given to us by the Wichita Broadcasters Association, our sponsor. Also, 75,000 free papers presenting our program and the gospel were handed out around the city. We then trained 200 counselors to talk to those making decisions at the meetings and held an open morning Bible study.

Friday and Saturday nights saw two concerts fea-

turing the Agajanian brothers, excellent country and western performers, and the Salt Company. Then for the next three nights I preached evangelistic sermons, preceded by lots of warm music led by Tom Rozof. By the time we were through, 10,000 had attended Century II, over 400 making recorded decisions for Christ with 80% of these being "first timers." Now 25 followup Bible studies dot Wichita.

Many remarked that the most impressive thing to them about "Five Days in June" was the Christian love shared by members of the team. Here were ex-drug addicts, athletes, musicians, professional people, "straights" and "long hairs," bound together in Jesus Christ. This is the maturing heart of the "Jesus Movement." Music again proved its role in communicating to masses of people. More than this, however, was the simple power of changed lives.

By June Tom's meetings now called BASIC ("Brothers and Sisters in Christ") were seeing 500 gather in the overcrowded church. An average of 15 were declaring their new faith in Christ weekly for a total of over 300 since Tom's ministry began. The free will offering was going to the struggling church, which more than 20 had already joined through BASIC. By fall, attendance zoomed to 700, and new converts were cleaning the church and volunteering to work in the black ghetto. Tom spent a week in Houston preaching nightly in a Presbyterian church, while other churches were looking for full-time leaders like Tom.

The spiritual explosion taking place in our nation today in and out of the established church has revealed one other need, a need represented by Tom.

A new kind of evangelist and communicator is arising without seminary training or ecclesiastical credentials. The only way to describe this leadership is that it is anointed by God. The initiative has passed beyond the professional Christian worker, whether he be pastor, youth leader, or campus-ministry staff member. Until now, youth evangelism has been inaugurated by adults. Now it comes from youth. The same hip teen-ager who last year turned his friends on to drugs may now be turning them on to Jesus. In an era when students have led the protest against war and racism, we should not be surprised that they have taken the gospel of Christ and moved it into their world. Tens of thousands evangelize today—rather than just a few paid professionals.

This presents the church with an awesome responsibility. These new leaders are entering the ministry and having results that would be the envy of any youth pastor. They have little theological or biblical training or sense of Christian history. They lack counseling skills. They have great faith, love, and passion for Christ and men. What are we to do with them? Are we to force them back into four years of college and three years of theological education, removing them from their culture for seven years, preparing them for a ministry which they already have? Absurd!

To place these new Christian leaders in at least some of our theological seminaries would be to reintroduce them to the intellectual games, the "mind trips," from which they have dropped out. Too often we have been guilty not only of dealing strictly in theological abstractions, but also of the failure to integrate mind and heart, thought and worship. The supposed "necessary" aloofness from human crisis for the sake of academic pursuit results in an unintended aloofness from divine power to answer that crisis.

Probing more deeply, the problem seems to come from a distorted understanding of education, based on classical models. We assume that learning takes place when the mind is stored with facts and theories, and the critical faculty is awakened to select among those facts or theories. We do not measure learning by observed behavioral change as does the Bible—"by their fruits you shall know them." The idolatry of our seminaries must also be confessed. Too often we have devoted ourselves to keeping up with the academic Joneses, another word for gaining and maintaining accreditation and having the seminary as intellectually respectable as any other graduate school.

What is needed now is a revamping of the entire process where education is seen as dealing with the whole man—mind, will and emotions—where acting out is essential, where learning is done by imitation and example, where Jesus' gathering a few men about him in intimate communion becomes our model again for turning the world upside down. These new leaders must have some of the tools which our older educational systems were designed to give to a different culture. But what they don't need are the artificial incentives of grades and exams in a tightly structured system. What they do need is a chance to learn in an intensely personal relationship with older believers who are studying and acting out with them the radical life called "Christian."

Thus at our church in the fall of 1971 a Center of Continuing Education was created to train this leadership. Verne, Devon, and Gary were among the first students. Lectures were supplied by a tape library. Daily seminars were organized on Old Testament, New Testament, theology, and counseling, with tutorials offered in remedial English and study habits, Greek, speech, and history. I became the first instructor, along with Dr. James Oraker in psychology and counseling. At least a third of the time each week was to be spent in acting out the learning in some form of ministry—not just "field work" on the weekends as most seminaries offer. A student may come for a month or a year and stay as long as he believes God wants him to be with us. At the same time cassette tapes and printed materials were created and collected to extend the teaching to other Christian groups scattered about.

Educational forms such as these must be created throughout the country to give the treasures of Christian knowledge to this called generation. Will we simply leave Tom in Wichita as his crowds and converts increase, or will we stand beside him to help shoulder the responsibility; this is the crisis and the opportunity which the Jesus Movement presents to the church. Hopefully, as we train its leadership, a more effective job will be done on the streets from which these new Christians have come. It's up to us.

7

challenge to the churches

We are now seeing the tragic collapse of the earlier idealism of the youth culture. If Dotson Rader is right in saying this is a generation of believers looking for a cause, we must conclude that most have failed to find it.

The musicians have stumbled. Bob Dylan became a recluse; the Beatles broke up; Jimi Hendrix, Janis Joplin, and Jim Morrison of the "Doors" are all dead from drugs. The Rolling Stones' hiring of the Hell's Angels for security at Altamont ended in violent death, as the post-Woodstock festivals became scenes of tragedy and despair. The gods fell from Mount Olympus, and the mere mortals below turned to the nostalgia of country and western music seeking the simplicity of an earlier age. The old words: hope, love, truth, peace, seem as illusive as Atlantis or Eldorado.

What of hope? The militant blacks now rejected the aid of white liberals and their student manpower in the civil rights struggle. The assassinations of the Kennedys and Martin Luther King left the nation in shock, and on the streets of Chicago at the Democratic Convention of 1968 hope for this generation died.

What of love? The carnival of Haight-Ashbury and Greenwich Village turned into the nightmares of hard drugs and prostitution as the criminal element wiped out the flower children. The violence, selfishness, and egotism of man, as well as his pathos and tragedy, were portrayed in films such as *Midnight Cowboy, Easy Rider,* and *Alice's Restaurant*—a common theme in all of them being death.

What of truth? The quest for truth was thwarted by excessive subjectivism and rebellion against absolutes. The psychedelics, designed to "expand" the mind, fell before the harder drugs of despair. The quest for many ended in nodding out in a euphoric fog.

What of peace? The age became ugly. Campus and ghetto riots were now justified as King was rejected for his non-violence. The Maoist form of revolution became "in" for the radical left; confrontation was designed to reveal the true violence of the establishment. This became the counsel of frustration, and for many that was all that remained.

Out of this death God is bringing a resurrection. From the ashes of the youth culture the old ideals have received a new basis in reality and a new content through Christ expressed in the Jesus Movement.

In the last three years, the West coast, the supposed center of sensual pleasure, has ironically reached a flash point of despair over this world and the spiritual longing for another.

The igniting of this spiritual fire has taken many forms: the political spark of the Christian World Liberation Front in Berkeley, offering an alternative to dominant Marxism; the Pentecostal spark of Calvary Chapel, a church context for wide revival; the youth culture spark of the Salt Company Coffee House in Hollywood, communicating to this generation in gospel-folk rock music; the communal spark of The Mesa in Palo Alto, and "Jesus parties" attended by hundreds of teen-agers; the militant spark of The Jesus Army in Seattle; the student ministry spark of The Light and Power House near UCLA; the hippie spark of several hundred youth forming The Church in the Park in Covina; the denominational spark of Lutheran Youth Alive; the underground-paper spark of the *Hollywood Free Paper* and many others.

Now a new generation of musicians is arising. Behind the commercialized *Jesus Christ, Superstar* and the "top forty" religious songs is a new and authentic Jesus music interpreting and expressing genuine

Christian experience. An example is the recent music of Paul Stookey, a member of one of the most enduring folk groups, Peter, Paul, and Mary. I first met Stookey during a taping for the Smothers Brothers Show in Hollywood about a month before his conversion. At that point he was reading the Bible seriously and asking many questions. His vibrant intense personality was earnestly looking for the real Christ, and he was not to be disappointed. Now his album, *Paul And* is filled with deeply biblical songs reflecting his vital relationship with Jesus.

The Love Song, The Salt Company, Larry Norman, and the recently converted commercial group, The Philharmonic, are creating a new world of Christian music, along with a host of others. Calvary Chapel in Costa Mesa boasts seven musical groups. Here is music arising from the youth culture and authentic Christian experience, rather than music being imposed upon it from older professionals. To listen to the music is to hear the Jesus Movement at its deepest moments. But what of the content?

What of hope? Hope has been redefined and restored. Based in the resurrection of Jesus Christ from the dead, hope is now both historically grounded and personal in "Christ our contemporary." Hope is a confidence in the future which belongs not to atomic destruction or ecological disaster but to Jesus Christ. Hal Lindsey's book, *The Late Great Planet Earth*, a best-seller on Biblical prophecy and the second coming of Christ, is in every Christian commune across the country. A speaker today can get the biggest crowd response by pointing heavenward and shouting that Jesus is coming again. The danger of this in excess is the loss of a sense of history and the abandonment of social responsibility by the "now" Christian. The New Testament maintains the tension, however, and so must we.

I have seen hope return to the face of Devon because of Jesus. I have seen him move to "mind-blown" addicts with that hope. I have heard the words of hope from Jon in his difficult rehabilitation from homosexuality. I myself experienced that hope in dealing with Mark when he was trapped in his drug haze. In Christ there is hope for now and eternity, and the longing of the youth culture is at last fulfilled.

What of love? Here is the heart of the gospel: God loves us and accepts us just as we are in Jesus Christ. Now we who are secure in that love are free to love ourselves, each other, and this world.

The quest for community is answered in the Christian body of believers. The communal ideal is being realized in thousands of living cells across the nation. At the Virgil House words such as "family" and "brother and sister" received a new lease on life. More than one person off the streets has confided, "This is the first family I have ever had."

The power of this love is overwhelming. Even at our lowest moments the "something extra" was there: people learning to listen, to care, to express their feelings; people accepting responsibility for themselves and others; people giving even when they didn't feel like it. The love of God was be-

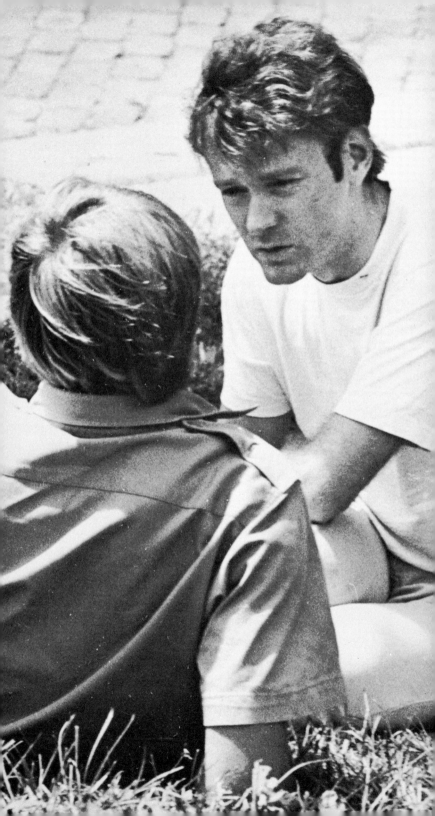

coming incarnate again, and the lonely and lost "wanted in."

The church was no longer seen as a building or an activity, but as a body, organic rather than organized. The 1500 year history of hierarchical Christianity where all spiritual power, life, and wisdom were focused in the priest or minister, was being reversed. That spiritual life was now experienced in the community where each member became an important part.

I am convinced that the greatest evangelistic impact does not come from the preacher or street witness or Christian coffee house, but from a committed body of believers living and working together. Jesus said that men would know of our discipleship by our love for one another; there is no better place for this to be acted out than in a home where the common life is shared. As Verne put it, "I came into a Christian house and into the love of Christ."

Only this love fulfills the longings of youth by its quality as selfless, giving, and forgiving. For them the cross is not an empty symbol but a vibrant reality, communicating that love where Christ took the garbage and misery of the world upon himself. As that love heals hearts, so it begins to heal the world.

When I first told Devon of the way the father embraced his returning son in Jesus' parable, Devon's cry was for his dad to do the same. Over a year later, after the final evening of our preaching mission in Wichita, I returned with Devon to his home.

About midnight I opened the living room door and found Devon and his family seated in a circle on the floor, holding hands and praying together. After their prayers Devon and his dad threw themselves into each other's arms and wept. Such is the power of Christ's love to heal and restore. When Jesus calls us to himself, he calls us to each other simultaneously, and in that double call his love is demonstrated to the world.

What of truth? For the Jesus Movement the most common symbol has become the upraised index finger and the cry, "One Way." Here the uniqueness of Jesus Christ is maintained, one absolute in a sea of relativity.

To claim that this return to authority is immature is arrogance. The return to absolutes comes from a profound spiritual experience of the life-changing power of Jesus Christ. That the young Christians are returning to a biblical theology and morality is a consequence of the fulfilling experience of Christ. It is also, for many, a result of the spiritual deadness of the older liberal and liturgical churches with their cultural compromises.

The issue of truth is again before us, but truth to be tested by experience. Most of these new Christians "take the Bible literally." What does this mean? It means, first of all, that they reject modern philosophy and theology which they feel are merely mental games, "head trips." If it is true that this is an irrational age, this is not all bad for evangelical Christianity. The doctrine of the Trinity and the two natures of Christ are not rational. Rationalism created an anti-supernatural bias and a destructive biblical criticism that have undermined the Christianity of several generations. Now biblical Christianity with its absolutes is again being taught and believed in the land. The quest for truth in its wholeness, thought and experience, is being satisfied in Jesus Christ.

What of peace? This final ideal, easily lost amidst the violence and egotism of our times, has found a new basis in the reconciliation Jesus offers between man and man as well as between man and God. Through the power of Christ a new integration of the self creates a new self-image. As a girl put it, "God loves me; I had better love me." This peace with oneself gives a freedom and release drugs could never offer.

We now see a new generation seeking to work out peace as an ideal in the culture. It is safe to say that the majority of these new Christians are tending toward pacifism. As one said, "I find it hard to be among the blessed peace makers in the turret of a Patton tank." What this will ultimately mean for society remains to be seen.

To summarize, in the intellectual sphere today we see the shattering of the scientific world view which has dominated western man for a century. The turn to mysticism, hallucinogenic drugs, astrology, black magic, Satan worship, and witchcraft all bear witness to the demise of the technological mindset. In the moral sphere we see the drift and destruction of relativism and hedonism. In the political sphere we see resignation and frustration. In the spiritual sphere we see the longing and quest which has given birth to the Jesus Movement. In this move-

ment we are faced with a moment unparalleled in twentieth century Christianity. As in the early decades of Christianity we see the Spirit of God breaking into lives and breaking out into society with an authentic demonstration of the power of the gospel.

This, then, raises several crucial questions for the institutional church.

First of all, is the adult Christian community mature enough and secure enough to be open, flexible, and creative to reach these new Christians? Will we find new words and new forms to express the reality of our faith, or merely cling to the comfortable and familiar? Are we really willing to love these new believers and literally embrace them and take them into our fellowship?

Secondly, will the church invest in the research necessary to reach this generation, at the grass roots? Will we listen to the culture and respond to what we hear? Can we set people free to fail as well as to succeed in this venture of experiment?

Thirdly, will we live the gospel of "justification by faith" rather than "justification by works" and offer to alienated youth the unconditional love of Jesus Christ? Or will we demand that they clean up before they come to us and therefore before they come to Christ?

Fourthly, will we allow our staff, our budget, and our buildings to be crucified with Christ, to be broken and invested in the world? Will we give up our success images of church building, budget, and attendance and accept the decentralization of the

92

church into smaller units of love and service in the community? If we try to save our church, Jesus promises that we will lose it.

Fifthly, will we accept the new leadership which God is raising up, and support it, accepting its spiritual credentials rather than demanding its denominational and academic credentials? Or will we say, as the early Jews did of the Apostles, that these are "uneducated, common men," but fail to recognize as the Jews did that they have *been with Jesus?*

Sixthly, will we create new training centers of apprenticeship education for this leadership, giving them our theology, Bible, and history, unstifled by grades and degrees?

A new stream of the Spirit is moving across the land. Untold thousands of youth are "turning on" to Jesus. They need to find the full body of Christ. They need to know of Christ's lordship over all of life. They need grounding in the Scriptures. Their gifts to us are zeal and love in true community. Can we receive from them and give to them? This decade of church history will be determined not by the success or failure of the National Council of Churches and the Consultation on Church Union, but by our response to the Jesus Movement.

Don Williams, pastor at Hollywood Presbyterian Church, was converted by Young Life when he was fifteen. A graduate of Princeton Seminary with a Ph.D. in New Testament from Union Seminary and Columbia University in New York, he is now well-known to readers of *Christianity Today, Faith at Work,* and *Presbyterian Life.* In his work of ministering to young people of the Jesus movement he has participated in several evangelistic campaigns: as Bible teacher for Lutheran Youth Alive Congresses in San Diego, San Antonio, San Francisco, and Denver; as leader of spiritual emphasis week at North Park College and Seminary in Chicago in January, 1972; and as leader of a city-wide evangelism campaign called "Five Days in June" in Wichita, Kansas, which was attended by over 10,000 people. And he was cited by the Los Angeles City Council for his ministry to youth especially in drug rehabilitation.

Photos by Paul Bowen